Trauma, A Love Story

AF417774

Samantha Neil

Trauma, A Love Story © 2022 Samantha
Neil

All rights reserved.

No part of this publication may be
reproduced, stored in a retrieval system, or
transmitted, in any form or by any means,
electronic, mechanical, photocopying,
recording or otherwise, without the prior
written permission of the presenters.

Samantha Neil asserts the moral right to be
identified as author of this work.

Presentation by *BookLeaf Publishing*

Web: www.bookleafpub.com

E-mail: info@bookleafpub.com

ISBN: 9789395756990

First edition 2022

DEDICATION

This book however is for Lesley, you know who you are and the role you played in my life and I can't thank you for the amount of light you've helped me find in myself and in the world again. I have regained so much thanks to you and the work you've taught me to put in.

ACKNOWLEDGEMENT

To my Tribe,

My Aries soul sister!, how do I even begin to explain how much you are a part of this book, from poetry slams online to our long drives and vent sessions. You are the balance to my universe. And I love you so much

Chad, you my darling have been a huge piece of my life since the very beginning. You've seen me through the darkest but you've never left my side, this book is a symbol of the beginning of our future, a milestone we are reaching together.

Diane and Garrett, I'm sorry for everything you've gone through but I am so proud of the people you've become in spite of my actions and the impact my absence left on you. I love you both so much and I will never stop learning and growing to be the best big sister I can for you.

Sadie, the girl who knows who she is and inspired more than one of my poems. How can I thank you, from supporting me and cheering me on, to cheering me up, to being my squish. I love you boo. Squish Squared forever.

and to John, my university hero. You see the world in a way no one else can. You maintain your kindness and passion in spite of your hardships. I admire that so much about you. You've suffered me at my worst too and I've put you through a lot. I'm sorry, I am hoping this makes up for things a bit.

To my family, my friends- here I am. It wasn't easy getting here. I doubt I made life easy on any of you from my neurotic antics to my overthinking and panic attacks. Loving me wasn't always easy but you did it anyway. Thank you to everyone who maintained their belief in me even when my choices made no sense.

PREFACE

Thank you, for anyone reading this, just thank you. You're officially one of the people who is helping my dream come true and I hope someday the words you read in this book help you reach into your own mind and accomplish dreams beyond what you thought possible.

Disclaimer: Some themes in this book touch upon triggering topics, it is important to remind yourself when reading this book, that the feelings expressed on these pages were as freeing, empowering and healing as they were painful. You are not alone, and if you find yourself struggling or relating to any of the themes in these poems, please remember the folks in your corner. Some types of darkness linger longer than others, but even in the longest nights you just need to find the stars, your tribe are your stars.

Torn

I once loved your face
Until I learned you had two
I can never replace
Time lost and wasted with you

I find myself torn
For how can I feel grief
When with you I am worn
Without you I feel relief

You call me fake
Because I stand tall
You can continue to take
While I continued to fall

You said all I do is lie
Because I walked away
And explained to you why
What else was there to say

Now you sit in your hate
Looking to hand me the blame
But it isn't my fate
To keep playing your game

I wanted to wish you well
While you wished me in pieces
But now you can burn in hell
As I flatten out the creases

I have found myself once more
And I'm free now without you
All the things you've hurt me for
Are meaningless, as you are now too

Words like knives

Words cut like knives into my skin
Carve the fears deeper within
Insecurities take hold, twist me around
I scream for help but can't make a sound

Knives and blades make more sense
Oh how I miss their painful essence
To bleed him free of me
It's all I need don't you see

It hurts ways I can't understand
That you still have the upper hand
Just one sentence shatters my core
We just need to talk once more

Nothing can be said that hasn't already
And around you I can never be steady
You broke every piece of my mind
And some pieces I hope to never find

But for now I let the pain flow
Heal now so I can grow
I'll be free of you yet
Even if the pain of your love I never forget

Unravel

I'm unraveling that voice
You left inside my head
I'm taking back my choice
To believe in words you've said

I'm bringing myself back
To the place I should be
This foundation won't crack
Just you wait and see

I'm freeing myself from you
From the toxic that you are
Becoming who I want to
But still you left a scar

You'll never be fully gone
From the mark you left behind
But when the dark welcomes dawn
It will be my voice in my mind

Dark kept light

I am the dark kept light
I can never make it right
the words never spoken
each promise forever broken

I can't erase this hate
can't forgive the pain
I won't forget the fear
Can't escape what's here

I am the broken child
of a cold far from mild
the daughter of despair
in search of the one to care

i can't see the light
I can't find my place
I can't reach my home
I can't I can't I CAN'T

I am left in this dark
wolves howl their mark
growl to strike their prey
and in darkness I stay

Yet I can still smile
yet i can still laugh
yet i can still hope
but I can't ever stay

I am the dark kept light
hope i make this right
I am the light kept dark
as wolves howl their mark

I shouldn't have to

I shouldn't have to say
It's not a good place to stay
If the bruises from yesterday
Were "just from horse play"

When your neighbor calls
About screams heard in the walls
After all the sweaters and shawls
Can't hide the marks from your "falls"

When you hide every single tear
From your loved one out of fear
And again, siren sounds near
You tell them what they want to hear

When nights that he's at his drunkest
And Police lock him up till breakfast
Are the nights you get the most rest
Time.
But "he's trying his very best"

He loves you in his own way
Are dangerous words to say
Stop living in fear every day
Get help... do your best to get away

A Day Like This

On days like this
I stand in my way
Inside I shout
But No one hears it

On days like this
I put on my best smile
I feel so tired
Like I'm falling back

On days like this
I look at myself
I see only my past
So I close my eyes

I don't want days like this
Slipping backwards
Losing myself again
But I need days like this

On days like this
I push a little more
I fight a little harder
And remind myself

That a day like this
Is just a day
And tomorrow
Doesnt have to be...

A day like this

My words

My words are new
They are kind and true
They free me from you
When you make me blue

My words are rare
Filled only with care
Yours got me nowhere
Mine get me everywhere

My words are here
Spoken without fear
For when you are near
My words you cannot hear

I speak my words to you
Like you asked me to
But again nothing new
You ignored me as you do

Undefined Strength

I am completely undefined
The words within me
Seem almost lost at sea
Cold with no home to find

I am a shadow in the light
Bringing you down again
every now and then
I feel you grab me tight

I am a light in the shadow
Bringing hope to fears
And feigning off tears
Just never let me go

I have become this way
Like you have asked
Completed every task
Lost in this very day

I am broken but whole
As strong as I am weak
Yet never at my peak
Still searching for my soul

The journey has been long
And will always be so
But this my dear I do know
That I'll always be strong

My strength in me is there
Even when I do not see
It is deep within me
Though I feel quite bare

Poison Words

spiralling oUt of cOntr0l
how did it come to this?!
words...words empty words
filled with poisons
loaded darts waiting to kill

I am the victim
   of my own words
of your words

I am an object
nothing more...
than a foolish whore

mistakes

all of it
        every word

a mistake
            another poison
waiting to kill me
and I am anticipating
                        the moment it does

the moment numbness sets me free
free from the things you've done to me.....

Sheltered Ocean Storms

I wish I could release the ocean from behind my
eyes
Wish I could shelter myself from your storm of
lies
Wish I could wipe your stain from my memories
But what you've done to me, no one ever sees

I wish they could see underneath my skin
So they can see the scars your words left deep
within
Even now the blood is dry and the real scars
faded
Caused by a sad inner child that I've always
hated

Turn back the clock, take all of the pain away
Bring the sunshine back to my life today
Fix the scars searing my body
Please…help me…somebody

I'm breaking from every point of view
Because of what she's been able to do
Somebody Strip away her power over me
Please for once let someone else see

May they Rescue me from this dark prison
Undrown me from my past pool of crimson
Uncut my skin, unbreak my spirit and replace
my soul
Someone please…make my shattered pieces
whole

Inner Child Cries

I wish I could release the ocean from behind my
eyes
Wish I could shelter myself from your storm of
lies
Wish I could wipe your stain from my memories
But what you've done to me, no one ever sees

I wish they could see underneath my skin
So they can see the scars your words left deep
within
Even now the blood is dry and the real scars
faded
Caused by love from a mother to the daughter
she hated

Turn back the clock, take all of the pain away
Bring the sunshine back to my life today
Fix the scars searing my body
Please…help me…somebody

I'm breaking from every point of view
Because of what she's been able to do
Somebody Strip away her power over me
Please for once let someone else see

May they Rescue me from this dark prison
Un-drown me from this shore of crimson
Uncut my skin, un-break my spirit and replace
my soul
Someone please…make my shattered pieces
whole

Hands

I am the victim of my own skin
As your eyes fill with greed
Diminished deep within
Beauty has a price indeed

I dream of blades once more
As your hands search me
A graceful little whore
Is all that's left to be

I dream of bleeding out
As you invade my body
Filling my mind with doubt
Of what the others will see

I am the victim of desire
Suicide runs through my head
Burning my thoughts like fire
But I sit and weep instead

What is left inside of me
When you take it all away
You've officially broken me
On this very specific day

You roam and you explore
I tell you to stop please
And you go for a little more
As you say I am but a tease

I will end it all…someday somehow
Your hands will no longer invade
This I promise you right now
I am not a game to be played

Faded Words

He said smile for me princess
It would please me ever so
He said I love you Sam
Don't forget, I always will

He said I'll protect you my love
If you would only let me
He said I know I can pull you back
From every time you've slipped away

He said we're together in all this
And I promise to never let you go
He said I love you with all that I am
And if I die, I will love you still

He said I'll do anything I'm capable of
To be forever just you and me
I'll give you the confidence you lack
To give more meaning to your day

So here I smile for him once more
To please him ever so much
I say I love you too
And as you, I too always will

I say I trust with you I will be okay
And I will hold on tightly to you
I am positive that you will catch me
Every single time that I should fall

But the time came
and you did not catch
what a shame
that you'd meet your match

I freed myself from you
and yourself from me
we were broken through and through
and I was the one brave enough to see

Side effects of you

Alive but not breathing
Hurt but not feeling
Walking but not standing
Awake but barely moving

I trusted you, I did
I held on to your lies
But I was just a kid
Believed you were wise

I held your hands
And felt secure
But as it stands
The truth was obscure

The things you did
The silence I kept
The truths I hid
The nights I wept

Hands meant to trust
Hurt me the most
Delusional with lust
How is this just

Beauty turned to beast
Sweet turned to poison
Those hands I miss least
For a very good reason

Dear Mind

Dear Mind...

I think I'm finally on my way to being okay
again

I'll still stumble,
I'll still fall
I'll still get things wrong

So if you don't mind, you need to come home
now. So that we can work together
I know you're lost somewhere in the darkness
You left for a no return trip on my train of
thoughts

Step into the shiny moments
Blow away the fog
Rest through the pain
Take the time you need
Tame the wild beasts

Make friends with the monsters, they were once
lost too

Find the light

And we will be ok
Let's be together

Not for the family who walked away
No not for the broken promises
And lost goodnight kisses
Not for the teachers who didn't believe
For the principals who gave up

We've learned what we could
It's time to teach ourselves to more than survive

Not for our friends who walked away
Nor for those who will run away

We don't need to convince anyone anymore

Let's just be OK
For ourselves
Not for anxiety
Not for depression

But for beating the odds
For overcoming statistics
Breathing under water
When we were seconds from drowning
Let's do it for those who have watched us
stumble

Who have watched us fall
Those who have dusted us off
Those who have seen truth when we thrive
Who believed what we couldn't
Let's thrive for the love we have
For the friends here to stay
Let's do this for the world
We are a gift worth sharing
So let's keep being who we are
Foot in front of the other

One deep breath after the next
Affirm, reaffirm
Solidify reality
Escape moments
They aren't who we are
Pave a steady road
Create new moments
Tomorrow will always be unknown
Let's take it one day at a time
One step at a time
Meet me dear mind
Meet me halfway
Let's work harder together
And let's finally be okay

Here I fall, as I stand

Here I fall, before I stand
yet ask for no one's hand
I die as I begin to live
with no more left to give

When I see you tomorrow
I shall smile with hidden sorrow
so that you never ask or say
is everything okay today

Now I cry, behind this smile
life goes on all the while
now I breathe with no air
just waiting to care
what will become of me
once the world starts to see
that I've failed to hide
the pain kept deep inside

Silence masks my screams
as I break at the seams
Hidden behind composure
as I search for my closure
I am as unknown to me

as I am have become to thee
I fade as I begin to shine
whispering to the world "I'm fine"
there is nothing to see
when you think of me
nothing left to feel
as it is never real
I hold my pieces together
as I shall now and forever
Living though I have died
for those broken like me inside

Chad

He reaches into my heart
And carries me away
To a brand new start
Of a brand new day

with hands I crave to hold
and how he makes me feel
he reaches into my soul
and I know his love is real

a desired touch of the lips
his kiss I've yet to taste
without him time slips
away like such a waste

memories we made ours
and memories yet to make
sitting and talking for hours
never once wanting a break

his voice, sweet yet pure
my heart is carried away
for once I am sure
true love has come my way

Inner Child

I know I can do anything
Just challenge me and I'll do it
You say that's so amazing
But there's really nothing to it
Dare me to try for the skies
Expect me to fall on my face
But the secret in my eyes
My one and only saving grace
Just give me a quick glance
You will get what I wanna say
she is my every chance
The dawn of my everyday
Watch me soar beyond the clouds
With her holding me to our heart
watch me get up before the crowds
get wowed away before I start
The secret is in our hand
We now have built that trust
That gives us reasons stand
And give the world the best of us

I'm sorry little me

Little one, be silent and be still
Listen here, stand strong stand tall
Voices heard so loud and shrill
Waiting to hear me jump or fall

Little one just trust in me
Take a chance once more
Listen to me and you will see
Something worth fighting for

I was silent and I was still
I thought I was strong and tall
But pain was waiting for the kill
To find me and take it all

I trusted in the voices
I took another chance
I've fallen without choices
In this endless sorrowed dance

So now I face the reality
Let all pains burn away
or take the penalty

of being alone each day

I'm sorry little me
for all we couldn't do
for all I failed to see
But I'm proud of you and me

Anxiety Monster

Anxiety Monster
He creeps up inside my chest
And squeezes my organs tight
He steals me away from my best
And I can't do anything right
He screams at me inside my head
Tells me that it's all so wrong
I say things I wish remained unsaid
Oh how I wish he and I could get along
The anxiety monster sneaks
And you're his before you know it
Sometimes his visits last weeks
Others it's easy to outgrow it
The anxiety monster is here
Testing my strength and heart
He plays at my every fear
And rips my strength apart

Unravel- Response to Anxiety Monster

Dear Anxiety Monster
I'm unravelling that voice
You left inside my head
Taking back my choice
To believe in the things you've said
I'm bringing myself back
To the place where I should be
This time, my foundation won't crack
Just you wait and see
I'm freeing myself from you
From the toxic that you are
Becoming now who I want to
Even though you've left this scar
You'll never be truly gone
Truth is in the mark you left behind
But when you decide to respawn
It will be my voice in control of my mind

www.ingramcontent.com/pod-product-compliance
Lightning Source LLC
Chambersburg PA
CBHW061318140726
47998CB00006B/2450